The
Parables
of
Jesus
in
Rhymes

What is the Kingdom of God Like?

Renata Walker

WestBow Press books may be ordered through booksellers or by contacting:

WestBow Press
A Division of Thomas Nelson & Zondervan
1663 Liberty Drive
Bloomington, IN 47403
www.westbowpress.com
1 (866) 928-1240

ISBN: 978-1-9736-7651-5 (sc)
ISBN: 978-1-9736-7652-2 (e)

Library of Congress Control Number: 2019915508

Print information available on the last page.

WestBow Press rev. date: 01/08/2020

WESTBOW
PRESS®
A DIVISION OF THOMAS NELSON
& ZONDERVAN

THE PARABLES OF JESUS IN RHYMES

What is the Kingdom of God Like?

CONTENTS

THE DISCIPLES CAME TO HIM AND ASK,

"WHY DO YOU SPEAK TO THE PEOPLE IN PARABLES?

HE REPLIED: "THE KNOWLEDGE OF THE SECRETS OF THE KINGDOM OF HEAVEN

HAS BEEN GIVEN TO YOU, BUT NOT TO THEM.

WHOEVER HAS, WILL BE GIVEN MORE AND HE WILL HAVE AN ABUNDANCE.

WHOEVER DOES NOT HAVE, EVEN WHAT HE HAS WILL BE TAKEN FROM HIM.

THIS IS WHY I SPEAK TO THEM IN PARABLES."

MATTHEW 13:5-8 MARK 4:3-8 LUKE 8:5-8 NIV

THE SOWER

MATTHEW 13:5-8; MARK 4:3-8; LUKE 8:5-8

A FARMER WENT TO PLANT THE SEED IN A FIELD
AND WALKING, DROPPED SOME ON THE GROUND.
IT DIDN'T TAKE LONG FOR THE HUNGRY BIRDS
TO QUICKLY EAT UP ALL THE GRAIN THEY FOUND.

SOME OF IT FELL IN ROCKY, SHALLOW SOIL
AND SPRANG UP FAST WITH A LITTLE SHOOT
BUT WHEN THE SUN CAME UP IT WITHERED FAST
NOT HAVING A STRONG, HEALTHY ROOT.

SEED THAT FELL AMONG THE THORNY WEEDS
CHOKED BY THEM WAS SOON GONE,
BUT THE GRAIN THAT FELL INTO GOOD SOIL
GAVE A CROP MORE PLENTIFUL THAN SOWN.

THE SEED IS THE WORD OF GOD'S KINGDOM,
AND FOUR TYPES OF GROUND WHERE IT FELL,
ARE THE DIFFERENT KINDS OF RESPONSES
THAT PEOPLE MAY HAVE TO THE GOSPEL.

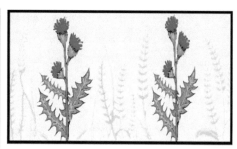

THE HARD GROUND IS A HEART HARDENED BY SIN.
THE MAN HEARS BUT DOES NOT UNDERSTAND IT
AND SATAN EASILY PLUCKS THE WORD AWAY
LEAVING THE HEART UNTOUCHED AND EMPTY.

THE STONY GROUND IS LIKE A WEAK BELIEVER
WHOSE FAITH IS STILL VERY SHALLOW
AND DISAPPEARS WHEN THE TROUBLE COMES
SINCE HIS HEART IS NOT YET READY TO FOLLOW.

THE THORNY GROUND IS LIKE A PERSON
SEEMINGLY RECEPTIVE TO GOD'S WORD
BUT THE SINFUL HEART AND THE TEMPTATIONS
TAKE HIM AWAY FROM THE TIME WITH THE LORD.

THE GOOD GROUND IS A STRONG BELIEVER
WHOSE HEART WAS TRULY CHANGED.
HE HEARS AND UNDERSTANDS THE GOSPEL,
PRODUCING THE SWEET FRUITS OF FAITH.

THE WEEDS (TARES)

MATTHEW 13:24-30

THE KINGDOM OF GOD IS LIKE A MAN
WHO WENT TO PLANT HIS WHEAT FIELD,
BUT THE ENEMY SOWN SOME BAD SEED IN BETWEEN
WANTING TO SPOIL THE FARMER'S GRAIN YIELD.

THE PUZZLED SERVANTS ALERTED THE OWNER
AFTER SEEING A LOT OF SPROUTING WEED.
"WHERE DID THE BAD TARES COME FROM?
WE PLANTED ONLY HEALTHY WHEAT SEED.

THE ENEMY DID THIS IN A DARKNESS OF NIGHT,
LET THEM GROW UNTIL THE HARVEST DAY.
YOU'D ROOT UP THE WHEAT BY PULLING TARES
TO SAVE THIS CROP YOU MUST DO AS I SAY."

AT THE TIME OF HARVEST GET ALL THE WEED,
THROW IT IN A FIRE WHEN THE TIME COMES.
GATHER THE GOOD GRAIN AND PUT IT ASIDE
LATER TO BE STORED SAFELY IN MY BARNS."

JESUS HIMSELF EXPLAINED TO THE DISCIPLES
THAT HE IS THE ONE WHO SOWS THE GOOD SEED
WHICH ARE ALL GOD'S FAITHFUL CHILDREN
IN THE WORLD THAT'S LIKE A FIELD OF WHEAT.

THE ENEMY SOWING THE BAD SEED IS SATAN
AND HIS CHILDREN, THE SINNERS, ARE THE WEEDS.
THE HARVEST WILL HAPPEN AT THE END OF TIME
WHEN THE WICKED WILL ANSWER FOR THEIR DEEDS.
THE HARVESTERS, GOD'S ANGELS WOULD COME
AND SEND THE SINNERS TO BURN IN HELL.
ALL THE RIGHTEOUS WILL SHINE LIKE A SUN,
AND IN HEAVEN THEY HAPPILY SHALL DWELL.

THE MUSTARD SEED

MATTHEW 13:31-32; MARK 4:31-32; LUKE 13:19

THE KINGDOM OF HEAVEN IS LIKE A TINY SEED
THE SMALLEST OF ALL THE SEEDS AROUND.
IT IS THE GRAIN OF THE PALESTINE MUSTARD
THAT MAN TAKES AND PLANTS IN THE GROUND.

THE MUSTARD SEED NEEDS ONLY ONE SEASON
TO GROW BIGGER, TALLER THAN ALL THE REST
AND BECOMES AS LARGE AS A SMALL TREE
WITH THE BRANCHES ON WHICH BIRDS CAN NEST.

JESUS IS THE SOWER, THE SEED IS HIS GOSPEL,
WHICH STARTED SMALL BUT GREW TO BE HUGE.
THE FIELD ARE HEARTS OF GOD'S FAITHFUL PEOPLE
TO WHOM THE GOSPEL OFFERS PEACE AND REFUGE.

THE YEAST (LEAVEN)

MATTHEW 13:33 LUKE 13:21

THE KINGDOM OF HEAVEN IS LIKE YEAST
THAT THE BREAD MAKER ADDS TO THE DOUGH.
YEAST MAKES THE BREAD LIGHT AND SOFT
BY CAUSING THE DOUGH TO RISE UP AND GROW.

JESUS' KINGDOM WAS SMALL AT THE BEGINNING
BUT SPREAD THROUGH THE WORLD LIKE WILDFIRES.
THE SAME WAY YEAST CHANGES THE DOUGH,
THE GOSPEL TRANSFORMS OUR HEA

WHEN WE ACCEPT CHRIST AS OUR SAVIOR
HIS GRACE IN US SLOWLY STARTS TO GROW
AND AFFECTS EVERYBODY AROUND US
LIKE A BIT OF YEAST CHANGES THE WHOLE DOUGH.

THE HIDDEN TREASURE

MATTHEW 13:44

THE KINGDOM OF HEAVEN IS LIKE A TREASURE
THAT A MAN FINDS COVERED DEEP WITH SAND.
HE'D BURY IT BACK NOT TELLING THE LANDOWNER
AND SELLS ALL HE HAS TO BUY THAT PIECE OF LAND.

THE KINGDOM OF HEAVEN HAS A GREAT VALUE
AND FINDING IT GIVES A SENSE OF PLEASURE
BUT IT REQUIRES FROM US TO GIVE UP A LOT
IN ORDER TO CLAIM THIS MUCH GREATER TREASURE.

THE PEARL OF GREAT VALUE

MATTHEW 13:45-46

THE KINGDOM OF HEAVEN IS LIKE A MERCHANT,
WHO IS LOOKING FOR FINE PEARLS AROUND
AND AFTER FINDING ONE OF GREAT VALUE
SELLS ALL HE HAS TO BUY THE ONE JUST FOUND.

IF WE WANT TO POSSESS THE HEAVENLY RICHES
WE MUST BE WILLING TO SACRIFICE THE WORLD.
THE GOSPEL COMES SOMETIMES WITH THE COST
WE MUST BE READY TO PAY, SAYS THE LORD.

THE NET

MATTHEW 13:47-50

THE KINGDOM OF HEAVEN IS LIKE A NET
THAT WAS LET DOWN INTO THE DEEP
CATCHING SEA CREATURES AND FISH OF ALL KIND,
SOME TO THROW AWAY AND SOME TO KEEP.

WHEN THE NET GETS FULL IT IS PULLED ON A BANK
AND THE MEN INSPECT ALL THE CAUGHT FISH.
PLACING SOME IN THE BASKET TO BE TAKEN HOME,
GOOD ENOUGH TO BECOME A DESIRABLE DISH.

THE USELESS, WORTHLESS ONES ARE THROWN AWAY
JUST LIKE WHEN OUR TIME COMES TO THE END,
THE ANGELS WILL COME TO CLAIM THE FAITHFUL,
AND THE WICKED INTO THE FIRE WILL BE SENT.

FINAL JUDGMENT IS TO SEPARATE US ALL,
SOME TO REWARD AND SOME TO PUNISH.
THE RIGHTEOUS WILL LIVE IN HEAVEN WITH GOD,
THE SINFUL IN THE PITS OF HELL WILL VANISH.

THE UNMERCIFUL SERVANT

MATTHEW 18:23-35

ONE DAY PETER CAME TO JESUS AND ASKED HIM:
"HOW MANY TIMES SHOULD I FORGIVE OTHERS?
WILL SEVEN TIMES BE A SUFFICIENT NUMBER
WHEN I AM WRONGED AND HURT BY MY BROTHERS?"

THE RABBIS TEACH TO FORGIVE THREE TIMES
BUT IF YOU BELONG TO THE KINGDOM OF HEAVEN,
YOU HAVE TO BE READY TO FORGIVE YOUR BROTHER
NOT SEVEN TIMES BUT SEVENTY TIMES SEVEN.

THE KINGDOM OF HEAVEN IS LIKE A KING
WHO WANTED TO COLLECT A DEBT
BUT THE SERVANT WHO OWED HIM A LOT
DID NOT HAVE THE MONEY TO PAY IT BACK.

ANGRY MASTER FOUND A QUICK SOLUTION
TO THE PROBLEM OF SETTLING THE LOAN:
"I WILL SELL YOU, YOUR WIFE AND THE CHILDREN"
THE SERVANT FELL ON HIS KNEES AT THE THRONE

"I BEG YOU, BE PATIENT WITH ME MY LORD
AND SOON I WILL PAY EVERYTHING I OWE!"
THE KING FELT SORRY FOR THE WEEPING SERVANT,
CANCELLED ALL HIS DEBT AND LET HIM GO.

A MAN OWED MONEY TO THE FORGIVEN SERVANT
WHO NOW DEMANDED, "GIVE BACK WHAT'S MINE!"
BUT THE POOR FELLOW COULDN'T PAY AND BEGGED:
"BE PATIENT WITH ME, I WILL NEED MORE TIME!"

THE SERVANT THREW HIM INTO DEBTORS JAIL
SINCE HE COULD NOT REPAY THE LOAN FASTER
SHOWING NO MERCY TO THE POOR, CRYING MAN
BUT OTHERS SAW AND TOLD THEIR MASTER.

HE CALLED THE SERVANT WHO CAME AS ORDERED
"YOU WICKED MAN, I FELT SORRY FOR YOU,
CANCELLED YOUR DEBT WHEN YOU BEGGED ME
AND YOU SHOULD SHOW MERCY TO YOUR DEBTOR TOO".

IN ANGER THE KING TURNED HIM OVER TO JAILER
UNTIL HE'D PAY WHAT WAS OWED FROM THE START
THIS IS HOW A JUST GOD WILL TREAT HIS SERVANTS
WHO DON'T FORGIVE OUT OF GOODNESS OF THE HEART.

YOU ARE THE SERVANT, SIN IS A DEBT, GOD IS THE KING
WHO DOESN'T PUNISH US FOR THE DEBT WE CAN'T REPAY
INSTEAD SHOWS A GREAT MERCY FORGIVING OUR SINS
AND WE HAVE TO TREAT OTHERS THE SAME WAY.

THE WORKERS IN THE VINEYARD

MATTHEW 20:1-16

THE KINGDOM OF HEAVEN IS LIKE A MAN
WHO HIRED WORKERS FOR HIS VINEYARD
PROMISING TO PAY EACH ONE DENARIUS,
A FULL DAY WAGE FOR WORKING HARD.

THREE HOURS LATER THE VINEYARD OWNER
DECIDED TO GO TO TOWN AND HIRE FEW MORE
AFTER SEEING SEVERAL IDLE MEN ON THE STREET
WHO SOON JOINED THE WORKERS HIRED BEFORE.

AFTER SIX HOURS, THEN NINE AND ELEVEN
THE LANDOWNER HIRED FEW MORE MEN AGAIN.
THEY ALL WENT TOGETHER TO THE FOREMAN
WHEN TIME TO COLLECT THEIR WAGES CAME.

FROM THE LAST HIRED, ENDING ON THE FIRST
THESE WHO WORKED HARD IN A HEAT ALL DAY
WERE PAID ONE DENARIUS AS THOSE WORKING LESS,
WHO RECEIVED FROM THE FOREMAN THE SAME PAY.

THE MEN COMPLAINED ABOUT THE UNFAIR WAGES
BUT THE LANDOWNER MADE IT CLEAR:
"YOU AGREED TO WORK FOR ONE DENARIUS
NO MATTER HOW MANY HOURS OTHERS WILL".

JESUS SAID MANY WHO ARE FIRST WOULD BE LAST
WHEN THE OLD PROPHESY SOON FULFILL
AND MANY WHO ARE LAST WOULD BE FIRST AT LAST.
GOD REWARDS HIS WORKERS ACCORDING TO HIS WILL.

SALVATION CANNOT BE EARNED, IT IS A FREE GIFT
GIVEN BY GOD'S GRACE AND NOT BY OUR MERIT,
AVAILABLE TO CLAIM FOR THE FOLLOWERS OF JESUS
AS WELL AS GREAT TREASURES OF HEAVEN TO INHERIT.

THE TWO SONS

MATTHEW 21:28-32

THE MAN ASKED HIS SONS TO WORK IN A VINEYARD
AND THE FIRST ONE WENT BUT AT FIRST SAID "NO"
THE SECOND SON ONLY PRETENDED TO BE OBEDIENT,
SAID "YES" TO HIS FATHER BUT HE DIDN'T GO.

WE OFTEN SAY "NO" TO THE LORD AT THE BEGINNING
BUT LATER WE OBEY SUBMITTING TO HIS WILL.
IT IS BETTER THAN BEING LIKE THE SECOND SON
AND MAKE A PROMISE WE DON'T MEAN TO FULFILL.

THE WICKED TENANTS

MATTHEW 21:33-46; MARK 12:1-12; LUKE 20:9-19

THE LANDOWNER PLANTED A VINEYARD
WITH A WATCHTOWER, A WINE PRESS, A WALL
AND WHEN IT WAS FINISHED, LEFT ON A JOURNEY
AFTER LETTING OTHERS LEASE IT ALL.

WHEN GRAPE HARVEST TIME ARRIVED
THE OWNER'S SERVANTS WERE SENT THERE
BUT THE TENANTS BEAT AND KILLED THEM ALL
RATHER THAN PAYING THE OWNER HIS SHARE.

TWICE MORE SERVANTS WENT THE NEXT TIME
WITH THE TASK TO COLLECT THE RENT
BUT WHEN THEY WERE TREATED VERY UNKINDLY,
THE OWNER'S ONLY SON WAS SENT.

THE WICKED TENANTS KEPT ALL THE PROFITS
AND KILLED THE VINEYARD OWNER'S SON
"WHAT WILL HE DO NEXT?" JESUS ASKED
"HE WILL MAKE THEM PAY FOR WHAT WAS DONE.

THE OWNER WILL DISTROY THE WICKED TENANTS
AND GIVE THE LAND TO OTHER FARMERS
WHO WOULD PRODUCE FRUIT AND PAY PROMPTLY
HIS SHARE OF THE CROP AT THE HARVEST."

THE WICKED TENANTS WERE THE JEWISH LEADERS
WHO KILLED THE PROPHETS AND WHEN IT WAS DONE
THEY PLANNED TO EXECUTE BY HANGING ON A CROSS
"THE CORNERSTONE" OF FAITH, GOD'S ONLY SON.

THE KINGDOM OF GOD WILL BE TAKEN FROM THEM
AND GIVEN TO OTHER, MORE FRUITFUL NATION,
TO PEOPLE WHO'D ACCEPT JESUS AS THEIR LORD
RECEIVE REDEMPTION AND THE GIFT OF SALVATION.

MARRIAGE OF KING'S SON

MATTHEW 22:1-14

THE KINGDOM OF HEAVEN IS LIKE A KING
WHO PREPARED A WEDDING FOR HIS SON
AND SENT THE SERVANTS TO TELL ALL INVITED
THAT IT IS THE RIGHT TIME NOW TO COME.

THE GUESTS REFUSED THE INVITATION TWICE
EVEN WHEN TOLD ABOUT THE FATTED CALF ROAST,
PLENTY OF WINE AND OTHER GREAT FOOD
PREPARED BY THE SERVANTS OF THE HOST.

ONE WENT TO HIS FIELD, ANOTHER TO HIS BUSINESS
AND THE SERVANTS WERE CAUGHT AND KILLED
SO, THE ANGRY KING SENT THE SOLDIERS INSTEAD
AS HIS HEART WITH DESIRE OF REVENGE WAS FILLED.

"THE GUESTS I INVITED DIDN'T DESERVE THE HONOR
TO ENJOY THE FEAST PREPARED FOR THEM ALL.
GO TO THE STREETS AND BRING WHOM YOU FIND
LET THE STRANGERS FILL MY BANQUET HALL."

THE SERVANTS DID WHAT THE MASTER ORDERED
AND HANDED A WHITE ROBE TO EVERY GUEST.
THEY ALL WORE IT PROUDLY EXCEPT FOR ONE MAN
WHO DID NOT PUT THE GARMENT ON, LIKE THE REST.

ON THE KING'S COMMAND HE WAS PUNISHED
BY BEING THROWN OUTSIDE INTO DARK NIGHT
LIKE EVERYBODY NOT DRESSED IN RIGHTEOUSNESS
WILL GNASH HIS TEETH AND WEEP IN FRIGHT.

GOD ASKED THE JEWS FIRST, THROUGH HIS PROPHETS,
BUT THEY REFUSED THE KING'S INVITATION.
PEOPLE GATHERED FROM THE STREET, THE GENTILES
ACCEPTED JESUS CHRIST AND RECEIVED SALVATION.

WE ALL HAVE TO WEAR THE PROPER GARMENT
WHICH IS THE CHARACTER OF JESUS, OUR HIGH PRIEST
AND PUT IT ON EVERY DAY BECAUSE WITHOUT IT
WE WILL NOT BE ALLOWED TO GO TO GOD'S FEAST.

RICH, POOR, YOUNG, OLD, SICK, BLIND OR CRIPPLE
THERE IS ROOM FOR EVERYONE AT GOD'S TABLE
WHO ACCEPT JESUS CHRIST AS THEIR SAVIOR,
WHO'D LIVE FOR HIM AND STAY FOREVER FAITHFUL.

THE TEN BRIDES

MATTHEW 25:1-13

WHAT IS GOD'S KINGDOM GOING TO BE LIKE?
WHEN THE END OF TIME WILL COME NEAR?
IT WILL BE LIKE TEN ANXIOUS BRIDES
WAITING FOR THEIR GROOM TO APPEAR.

THEY ALL WENT OUT CARRYING THEIR OIL LAMPS,
FIVE HAD SOME EXTRA OIL AND FIVE HAD NOT
BUT IT WAS LATE, THEY WERE TIRED OF WAITING
FELL ASLEEP AND WOKE UP AROUND MIDNIGHT.

THEY HEARD THAT THE GROOM WAS NEAR
AND TURNED THEIR LAMPS ON TO SEE HIM.
FIVE OF THE LAMPS WOULD GIVE THE LIGHT
BUT THE LAMPS OUT OF OIL WENT DIM.

THE FOOLISH GIRLS ASKED THE WISE ONES
"GIVE US SOME OF YOUR OIL, OUR LAMPS ARE DOWN!
WE CAN'T, THERE IS NOT ENOUGH FOR ALL OF US
GO AND BUY SOME OIL FOR YOURSELVES IN TOWN."

THE GROOM CAME WHEN THE GIRLS WERE GONE
AND NOT BEING THERE, HIS ARRIVAL THEY MISSED
BUT THE WAITING BRIDES WITH THE WORKING LAMPS
WERE TAKEN BY THE GROOM TO THE WEDDING FEAST.

LATER THE OTHER GIRLS CAME BUT THE DOOR WAS SHUT
AND THEY KNOCKED BEGGING "PLEASE, LET US IN!"
THE GROOM WOULDN'T LET THE FOOLISH BRIDES ENTER
"I DON'T KNOW YOU, WHERE HAVE YOU BEEN?"

SINCE WE DON'T KNOW THE DAY OR THE HOUR
WHEN JESUS COMES FOR THE CHURCH, HIS BRIDE,
WE ALWAYS HAVE TO BE READY TO MEET HIM
AND LIVE FOREVER IN HEAVEN BY HIS SIDE.

THE TALENTS

MATTHEW 25:14-30

A LAND OWNER WAS GOING ON A LONG TRIP
AND PUT HIS THREE SERVANTS IN CHARGE
GIVING THEM SOME MONEY TO MANAGE FOR HIM
EXPECTING HIS INVESTMENT TO GROW LARGE.

THE FIRST ONE USED MASTER'S RICHES WELL
AND THE FIVE TALENTS HE RECEIVED TO INVEST
SOON GREW TO TEN, DOUBLING THE VALUE
AS HE PASSED THE STEWARDSHIP TEST.

THE SECOND SERVANT JUST LIKE THE FIRST
FAITHFULLY FACED THE CHALLENGE
AND DOUBLED THE MONEY GIVEN BY THE MASTER
FROM THE TWO HE INVESTED TO FOUR TALENTS.

THE SERVANT WHO RECEIVED ONLY ONE TALENT
INSTEAD OF INVESTING HID IT IN A GROUND
TILL THE MASTER CAME BACK FROM THE TRIP
AND CALLED THEM TO SETTLE THE ACCOUNT.

THE FIRST AND SECOND FAITHFUL SERVANT
RECEIVED PRAISE AND REWARD FROM THE MASTER
BUT THE THIRD WAS CALLED LAZY, WICKED
AND THROWN OUT WEEPING IN THE DARKNESS.

FOR EVERYTHING WE HAVE IS GIVEN TO US BY GOD
WE CAN INCREASE IT AND SHARE GOD'S JOY
OR WE CAN JOIN THOSE WHO WASTE IT
AND WHOM AT THE END GOD WILL DESTROY.

"WELL DONE GOOD AND FAITHFUL SERVANT"
IS WHAT WE WANT TO HEAR ON THE LORD'S DAY
WHEN WE ARE PRAISED AND REWARDED
BEING GOOD STEWARD WHO LISTEN AND OBEY.

THE SEED GROWING GRADUALLY

MARK 4:26-29

THE KINGDOM OF GOD IS LIKE A MAN
WHO SCATTERS SEED ON A GROUND
AND NIGHT AND DAY THE SEED GROWS,
HE SEES IT BUT DOES NOT KNOW HOW.

ALL BY ITSELF SOIL PRODUCES GRAIN
THE STALK, THE HEAD, THE KERNELS
AND AS SOON AS THE GRAIN IS RIPE
THE FARMER IS READY FOR THE HARVEST.

GOD'S WORD IS SOWN IN OUR HEARTS
AND EVEN THOUGH THE PROCESS MAY BE SLOW
IT WILL PRODUCE THE FRUIT SOONER OR LATER
AS OUR FAITH WITH TIME MUST GROW.

THE TWO DEBTORS

LUKE 7:41-43

TWO MEN OWED MONEY TO THE SAME BANKER
BUT NEITHER OF THEM COULD REPAY THE DEBT
ONE OWED A LITTLE, ONE OWED MUCH MORE
AND THEY CAME TO THE BANKER VERY UPSET.

HE MERCIFULLY CANCELLED THE DEBT OF BOTH MEN
ONE WHO OWED MORE, ONE WHO OWED LESS
AND THEY WERE VERY GRATEFUL TO HIM
FOR THIS UNSELFISH ACT OF FORGIVENESS.

JESUS THAN ASKED SIMON THE QUESTION
"WHICH ONE OF THEM WILL LOVE HIM MORE"
AND SIMON ANSWERED CORRECTLY AS EXPECTED
"THE ONE WHO HAS A LOT TO BE FORGIVEN FOR"

THE GOOD SAMARITAN

LUKE 10:25-37

"YOU MUST LOVE GOD WITH ALL YOUR HEART,
ALL YOUR MIND, ALL YOUR STRENGTH AND SOUL,
LOVE YOUR NEIGHBOR AS YOURSELF" SAID JESUS
"IF INHERITING THE ETERNAL LIFE IS YOUR GOAL."

"BUT WHO IS MY NEIGHBOR" ASKED THE LAWYER
AND JESUS ANSWERED WITH THE STORY HE TOLD
ABOUT A TRAVELING MAN ATTACKED BY ROBBERS,
BEATEN AND LEFT HALF DEAD ON A ROAD.

THE PRIEST SAW HIM AND DID NOT STOP
INSTEAD CROSSED TO THE OTHER SIDE,
AND THE LEVITE SOON PASSED BY
NOT CARING THAT A MAN WAS ABOUT TO DIE.

THE HATED BY THE JEWS SAMARITAN
FELT SORRY FOR THE WOUNDED STRANGER
AND TOOK CARE OF THE MAN'S WOUNDS
KNOWING HIS LIFE WAS IN DANGER.

THE SAMARITAN TOOK THE MAN TO THE INN
BY PUTTING HIM ON A DONKEY TO RIDE
AND TENDED TO HIS WOUNDS TILL THE NEXT DAY
WHEN HE HAD TO LEAVE THE HURT STRANGER'S SIDE.

THE INNKEEPER WAS PAID TO LOOK AFTER HIM
EVEN SO THE SAMARITAN HAD NO MONEY TO SPARE
BUT HE PROMISED TO RETURN AND PAY EVEN MORE
TO COVER THE COST OF THE WOUNDED MAN'S CARE.

"WHO WAS THE NEIGHBOR" JESUS ASKED THE LAWYER
"TO THE MAN ATTACKED BY THE ROBBERS?
THE ONE WHO HAD MERCY ON HIM" HE ANSWERED
"THEN GO AND BE LIKE HIM TOWARD OTHERS."

THE FRIEND AT MIDNIGHT

LUKE 11:5-8

ONE OF THE DISCIPLES ASKED JESUS:
"PLEASE TEACH US MASTER HOW TO PRAY"
AND JESUS TOLD THEM THE LORD'S PRAYER
"THIS IS HOW I DO I, THIS IS THE RIGHT WAY".

THE MAN KNOCKED AT THE DOOR OF A FRIEND
"PLEASE LET ME BORROW SOME BREAD
I HAVE A GUEST AND NOTHING TO EAT,
OPEN THE DOOR AND DON'T BE MAD.

IT'S LATE, DON'T BOTHER ME" HE MAY SAY
"THE DOOR IS LOCKED, MY FAMILY IS IN BED
I CAN'T GET UP, IT IS AFTER MIDNIGHT,
NOT A GOOD TIME TO ASK FOR BREAD."

INSTEAD HE WILL SAY "YES" TO THE BOLD REQUEST
BECAUSE OF THE PERSISTENCE OF HIS PLEA
AND NOT BECAUSE HE IS A GOOD FRIEND
BUT BECAUSE OF THE HUMBLY BENDED KNEE.

"ASK AND IT WILL BE GIVEN TO YOU" JESUS SAYS
"EVERYONE WHO ASKS WILL SURELY RECEIVE,
SEEK AND YOU WILL FIND IT IS A PROMISE
KNOCK AND THE DOOR WILL OPEN IF YOU BELIEVE."

THE RICH FOOL

LUKE 12:16-21

A RICH MAN'S LAND PRODUCED VERY GOOD CROP
BUT THERE WAS NOT ENOUGH ROOM FOR IT ALL
AND STORING THE HARVEST BECAME A PROBLEM
SINCE THE OLD BARNS WERE MUCH TOO SMALL.

HE DECIDED TO BUILD THE NEW, BIGGER BARNS
WITH ENOUGH ROOM TO STORE HIS GRAIN
AND TAKE IT EASY, EAT, DRINK, BE MERRY,
TO THE FULLEST ENJOYING HIS WEALTH AND GAIN.

GOD CALLED THE LANDOWNER THE SELFISH FOOL
"YOU HAVE AN EARLY RETIREMENT PLANNED
BUT THERE WON'T BE TIME TO ENJOY THE WEALTH
BECAUSE THAT NIGHT YOUR LIFE WOULD END."

GOD BLESSES US TO FURTHER HIS KINGDOM
THIS IS THE TRUTH THIS STORY TEACHES.
WE ARE BLESSED TO BE BLESSING TO OTHERS
AND LIFE IS NOT ABOUT GATHERING RICHES.

THE BARREN FIG TREE

LUKE 13:6-9

A MAN HAD A FIG TREE IN HIS VINEYARD
WHICH FRUITLESSNESS MADE HIM VERY ANNOYED.
IT DIDN'T PRODUCE ANY FIGS FOR THREE YEARS
AND HE ORDERED THAT IT WILL BE DESTROYED.

THE HOPEFUL KEEPER ASKED HIM TO WAIT
KNOWING THAT WITH FERTILIZER AND CARING
IN JUST ONE YEAR THIS NON-PRODUCTIVE TREE
MAY FLOURISH AND BECOME FRUIT BEARING.

GOD GIVES US THE RIGHT NOURISHMENT,
PLENTY OF TIME AND ROOM TO GROW,
BUT HIS MERCIFUL PATIENCE HAS ITS LIMITS
WHEN THE FRUITS OF OUR FAITH DON'T SHOW.

WHEN WE ARE LIVING AS A PART OF GOD'S PURPOSE
HE GIVES US TIME TO DEVELOP OUR FAITH
BUT IF WE DON'T START PRODUCING FRUIT
HE'D CUT US DOWN LIKE A TREE TAKING UP A SPACE.

THE GREAT SUPPER

LUKE 14:16-24

A CERTAIN MAN INVITED MANY GUESTS
TO THE GREAT FEAST HE WAS PREPARING
AND SENT A SERVANT TO TELL THEM IT WAS READY
BUT THEY IGNORED IT, DISMISSIVE AND UNCARING.

THE HOST TOLD HIS SERVANT TO INVITE OTHERS
THE POOR, THE CRIPPLED, THE LAME, THE BLIND
AND FILL THE BANQUET HALL WITH STRANGERS,
JUST ANYBODY FROM THE STREET HE COULD FIND.

NONE OF THE FIRST INVITED GUESTS
WHO HAD UNWISELY CHOSEN NOT TO ATTEND,
WILL BE ASKED AGAIN TO JOIN THE FEAST
WHEN THEIR TIME WILL COME TO THE END.

THE BLESSINGS OF HEAVEN ARE WAITING
FOR THOSE WHO ACCEPT LORD'S INVITATION
AND COME TO JOIN CHRIST AT HIS TABLE
THROUGH THE OPEN DOOR OF SALVATION.

THE LOST SHEEP

MATTHEW 18:12-14; LUKE 15:4-7

IF A MAN OWNS A HUNDRED SHEEP
AND ONE OF THEM WANDERS AWAY
HE'D LEAVE THE NINETY- NINE ON THE HILLS
AND LOOK FOR THE LOST ONE, NIGHT OR DAY.

HE IS HAPPIER ABOUT THE FOUND SHEEP
THEN ABOUT THE REST THAT DIDN'T GO ASTRAY
THE SAME WAY GOD WILL SEEK LOST SOUL
HAPPY TO BRING HIM HOME, READY TO OBEY.

THE LOST COIN

LUKE 15:8-10

IF THE WOMAN LOSES ONE SILVER COIN
SHE'D LIGHT THE LAMP, SWEEP THE FLOOR
AND SEARCH UNTIL IT IS FOUND
EVEN THOUGH SHE HAS NINE MORE.

WHEN SHE FINDS THE MISSING COIN
SHE WILL TELL EVERYBODY AROUND
FULL OF RELIEF AND JOY AT LAST
THAT HER LOST TREASURE WAS FOUND.

THE SAME WAY ANGELS REJOICE IN HEAVEN
AND CALL FOR A BIG CELEBRATION
EVEN WHEN ONE SINGLE SINNER REPENTS
FOLLOWING OUR LORD'S INVITATION.

THE PRODIGAL SON

LUKE 15:11-32

THERE WAS A MAN WHO HAD TWO SONS
AND ONE OF THEM TOLD THE FATHER ONE DAY
"LET ME HAVE A PART OF THE ESTATE
WHICH WOULD BE MINE IN A FUTURE ANYWAY."

THE FATHER DID AS THE SON REQUESTED
EVEN THOUGH HE WAS HURT AND SAD.
SOON AFTER THAT, THE YOUNG MAN LEFT
TAKING WITH HIM ALL THE POSSESSIONS HE HAD.

HE WENT TO A FAR AWAY COUNTRY
WHERE HIS MONEY DID NOT LAST LONG
SPENT ALL ON SINFUL, WILD LIVING
AND SOON THINGS STARTED TO GO WRONG.

WITH NOTHING LEFT TO MAKE A LIVING
AND SEVERE FAMINE IN THE LAND
HE FOUND HIMSELF IN NEED OF A JOB
BECOMING A PIG FARMER'S HIRED HAND.

STARVING HALF TO DEATH ALL THE TIME
WHILE TENDING TO THE HERD OF SWINE
MADE HIM TO GO BACK TO THE OLD LIFE
AND THE FAMILY HE LEFT BEHIND.

THE FATHER SAW THE YOUNGER SON COMING
WHEN HE WAS STILL FAR AWAY
AND HIS HEART FILLED WITH LOVE KNEW THEN
THAT HIS SON IS COMING BACK TO STAY.

HE STARTED RUNNING TOWARD HIM
FULL OF COMPASSION AND JOY,
THROWING HIS ARMS AROUND THE SON
KISSED AND WELCOMED HIS BELOVED BOY.

"I HAVE SINNED AGAINST GOD AND YOU,
I AM NOT WORTHY TO CARRY YOUR NAME
LET ME STAY HERE AS YOUR SERVANT
TO BEING YOUR SON I HAVE NO CLAIM."

BUT INSTEAD THE SERVANTS WERE ORDERED
THE BEST ROBE FOR HIS SON TO BRING,
NICE SHOES FOR HIS TIRED, BARE FEET
AND FOR HIS FINGER THE FAMILY RING.

WHEN THE WELCOME PARTY STARTED
THE OLDER SON CAME HOME FROM THE FIELD
ASKING ABOUT THE MUSIC AND LAUGHTER,
THE REASON FOR THE FEAST WAS REVEALED.

HE GOT ANGRY AND REFUSED TO GO IN
"I DON'T UNDERSTAND WHAT IS SO GREAT
ABOUT MY SINFUL BROTHER'S RETURNING
AFTER WASTING AWAY PART OF OUR ESTATE!

THERE WERE NO PARTIES THROWN FOR ME
LIKE FOR MY BROTHER WHO LOST ALL HE HAD.
I WAS OBEDIENT AND WORKING HARD,
HE LEFT WHEN I STAYED HELPING OUR DAD."

THE FATHER SAID TO HIM:"MY DEAR SON
I LOVE YOU AND I AM REALLY GRATEFUL
BUT I AM HAPPY SEEING HIM SAFE AND SOUND
EVEN THOUGH HE WAS UNFAITHFUL.

MY SON IS ALIVE AND HE WAS DEAD
HE IS NOW FOUND BUT HE WAS LOST
HE HAS REPENTED AND I FORGAVE HIM
HE IS SORRY FOR WHAT HIS SINS HAD COST."

GOD EMBRACES US WHEN WE COME BACK HOME
AND WASHES AWAY THE SINS OF OUR PAST
WE RECEIVE HIS GRACE, HIS FORGIVENESS
COMING FROM UNEARNED LOVE FOR US.

THE SHREWD MANAGER

LUKE 16:1-9

THE MANAGER WORKING FOR A RICH MAN
WAS MISHANDLING BUSINESS OF HIS MASTER
AND SHOWING HIM THE BOOKS AS REQUESTED
WOULD HAVE BEEN A REAL DISASTER.

THE MANAGER SCARED OF LOSING HIS JOB
AND BEING A QUICK-THINKING MAN
NOT WANTING NOR ABLE TO DO OTHER WORK
CAME UP WITH A CLEVER BUSINESS PLAN.

HE WENT TO SEE HIS MASTER'S DEBTORS
HOPING TO TURN EACH OF THEM INTO A FRIEND
WHOM HE COULD DEPEND ON BEING HELPFUL
WHEN HIS MANAGING JOB WOULD END.

"HOW MUCH DO YOU OWE MY MASTER?
I AM READY TO OFFER YOU THIS GREAT DEAL
AND CUT YOUR DEBT TO HALF WHAT YOU OWE
BUT REMEMBER THIS IS OUR FRIENDSHIP SEAL.

EIGHT HUNDRED GALLONS OF OLIVE OIL
I CHANGE TO FOUR HUNDRED" HE SAID
"A THOUSAND BUSHELS OF WHEAT
I WRITE AS EIGHT HUNDRED INSTEAD"

THE MANAGER GAVE UP HIS OWN PROFIT
WHICH WAS EQUAL TO THE GIVEN DISCOUNT
AND THE LOANS WERE MUCH EASIER TO REPAY
BROUGHT DOWN TO THE INITIALLY OWED AMOUNT.

NO LONGER OVERCHARGED DEBTORS WERE GLAD,
THE MASTER PRAISED HIM FOR BEING SHREWD
BUT JESUS CALLED THE STEWARD'S ACTIONS SINFUL
AND CONDEMNED HIS MORALLY WRONG ATTITUDE.

THERE IS MORE TO LEARN FROM THIS STORY
WHAT WE NEED TO KEEP IN OUR MIND
LIKE PAYING ATTENTION TO THE THINGS IN LIFE
THAT ARE TEMPORARY BUT VITAL TO HUMANKIND.

THOSE WHO LEARN TO WISELY TAKE CARE
OF THEIR EARTHLY AFFAIRS AND NEEDS
WILL MANAGE THEIR FAITH WITH WISDOM
AND OBEDIENTLY PLANT SPIRITUAL SEEDS.

BE FRIENDS RATHER THAN ENEMIES WITH THOSE
WHO HAVE AUTHORITY, WEALTH AND POWER,
THEY MAY BE OF HELP TO THE RIGHTEOUS SOMEDAY
WHEN WE NEED IT IN OUR LIFE'S DARKER HOUR.

THE RICH MAN AND LAZARUS

LUKE 16:19-31

A VERY RICH MAN LIVED IN COMFORT,
HAD NICE CLOTHES AND PLENTY TO EAT
UNLIKE POOR LAZARUS THE BEGGAR
WHO LAID BY HIS GATE IN THE STREET.

LAZARUS SPENT HIS DAYS WAITING
FOR THE SCRAPS FALLEN FROM THE TABLE
AND THE RICH MAN HAD NO COMPASSION
FOR THE NEEDY, POOR, SICK OR DISABLED.

LAZARUS DIED AND WAS TAKEN TO HEAVEN
BUT THE RICH MAN'S SOUL WENT TO HELL
PUNISHED FOR BEING UNREPENTANT SINNER
IS WHERE HE WOULD FOREVER DWELL.

HE BEGGED ABRAHAM:" SEND DOWN LAZARUS
WITH A DROP OF WATER TO RELIEVE MY THIRST."
"YOU HAD ALL THE GOOD THINGS" ABRAHAM SAID
"BUT WOULDN'T SHARE SO NOW YOU ARE CURSED"

THOSE TAKEN TO HEAVEN DON'T COME DOWN
AND THOSE SENT TO HELL MUST STAY THERE
NO ROAD CONNECTING BOTH PLACES WAS BUILD
SO, THIS IS YOUR DESTINY FOREVER TO BARE.

"THEN PLEASE SEND LAZARUS BACK TO EARTH
TO WARN MY FIVE SINFUL BROTHERS.
I DON'T WANT THEM END UP IN THIS PLACE
SUFFERING LIKE ME AND ALL THE OTHERS."

ABRAHAM ANSWERED "THEY DON'T BELIEVE
IN WHAT MOSES AND THE PROPHETS SAID
THEY WILL NOT LISTEN TO LAZARUS' WORDS
EVEN AFTER HE RAISES FROM DEAD."

THERE IS NO SECOND CHANCE AFTER DEATH
DON'T BE COLD HEARTED AND FULL OF GREED
"NO MERCY GIVEN, NO MERCY RECEIVED"
SO BE SENSITIVE TO THOSE IN POVERTY AND NEED.

THE UNWORTHY SERVANTS

LUKE 17:7-10

A SERVANT WHO FINISHED PLOWING A FIELD
OR LOOKING AFTER THE MAN'S SHEEP
DOESN'T COME HOME EXPECTING REWARDS,
TIME TO RELAX, EAT AND GO TO SLEEP.

THE SERVANT HAS TO GO ON HELPING HIS MASTER
UNTIL DISMISSED AND ALLOWED TO REST
FOLLOWING WHAT HE IS TOLD TO DO
AND NOT FOR THE MASTER TO BE IMPRESSED.

WE HAVE TO ANSWER A CALL TO SERVE
USING GOD'S GIVEN GIFTS AND ABILITY
FOR HE IS THE ONE WHO APPOINTS OUR DUTIES
AND WE NEED TO ACCEPT THEM WITH HUMILITY.

THE PERSISTENT WIDOW

LUKE 18:1-8

TO A JUDGE WHO DID NOT FEAR GOD
NOR CARED ABOUT HIS FELLOW MEN
A POOR WIDOW KEPT ON COMING BACK
PLEADING FOR HELP AGAIN AND AGAIN.

SHE HAD A COMPLAINT AGAINST SOMEONE
AND WANTED JUSTICE FROM THE JUDGE
BUT HE WOULD NOT GRANT HER REQUEST
STUBORN AND HEARTLESS, WOULD NOT BUDGE.

THE JUDGE KEPT ON REFUSING HER PETITION
BUT THE STUBBORN WIDOW GOT HIM TO AGREE
BY WEARING HIM DOWN TO THE POINT
THAT HE LISTENED AND ANSWERED HER PLEA.

AFTER SHE KEPT ON ASKING FOR HELP
EVEN THIS UNCARING MAN WOULD LISTEN.
SURELY OUR LOVING GOD WILL ANSWER
IF WE PRAY WITH FAITH AND WITHOUT CEASING.

THE PHARISEE AND THE TAX COLLECTOR

LUKE 18:10-14

A TAX COLLECTOR AND THE PHARISEE
WENT TO THE TEMPLE TO PRAY.
THE PHARISEE PRAYED STANDING PROUDLY
WITH HIS SELF- RIGHTEOUSNESS ON DISPLAY.

"THANK YOU GOD THAT I AM NOT A SINNER
RATHER A WALKING FAITHFULNESS EXAMPLE.
I FOLLOW YOUR LAWS, FAST TWICE A WEEK
GIVE A TENTH OF MY MONEY TO THE TEMPLE."

THE TAX COLLECTOR'S PRAYER WAS DIFFERENT
AS HE STOOD WITH HIS HEAD KEPT LOW
BEAT THE CHEST WITH A GREAT REMORSE
AND LET ALL THE SHAME WITH HIS TEARS FLOW.

"GOD HAVE MERCY ON ME A SINNER" HE PRAYED
AND RECEIVED GRACE FOR ALL HIS FAULTS.
GOD HUMBLES THOSE WHO EXALT THEMSELVES
AND THOSE WHO ARE HUMBLE, HE EXALTS.

THE POUNDS (MINAS)

LUKE 19:12-27

THE SERVANTS OF A CERTAIN NOBLE MAN
WHO FOR A WHILE HAD TO LEAVE HIS DOMAIN
WERE GIVEN AN EQUAL SUM OF THE TALENTS
TO WISELY INVEST FOR THE FUTURE GAIN.

HE WENT AWAY TO BE APPOINTED A KING
AND IT HAPPENED JUST AS PLANNED
EVEN THOUGH NOBODY WANTED HIM TO RULE
THE LORD WAS READY TO TAKE CHARGE OF HIS LAND.

HE CAME BACK AND CALLED HIS TEN SERVANTS
TO FIND OUT HOW MUCH THEY'VE EARNED.
THE FIRST ONE GREW THE ASSETS TO TEN MINAS
SO, THE KING WAS PLEASED WHEN HE LEARNED.

"WELL DONE MY GOOD, FAITHFUL SERVANT
I GIVE YOU TEN CITIES FOR DOING SO FINE
AND YOU, WHO EARNED FOUR MINAS FOR ME
GET TO BE IN CHARGE OF FIVE CITIES OF MINE."

THE THIRD MAN BROUGHT JUST ONE MINA,
THE SAME AMOUNT HE RECEIVED TO GROW
AS HE KEPT IT HIDDEN AFRAID TO LOSE IT
AND DID NOT REAP WHAT HE DID NOT SOW.

HE CALLED THE MASTER TOO DEMANDING
AND PLEASING HIM AN IMPOSSIBLE THING
SO, THE WASTED TALENTS WERE TAKEN AWAY
TO BE GIVEN TO THE ONE WHO REVERED HIS KING.

''HE WHO HAS NOTHING WILL LOSE WHAT HE HAS
HE WHO HAS SOME WILL BE GIVEN MORE
AND THOSE WHO DON'T ACCEPT ME AS THEIR KING
WILL BE PUNISHED WHEN WE SETTLE THE SCORE.''